A Guide
Beaches ar
of Dorset

by Robert Hesketh

Inspiring Places Publishing
2 Down Lodge Close
Alderholt
Fordingbridge
SP6 3JA
www.inspiringplaces.co.uk

This reprint 2017
ISBN 978-0-9564104-6-7

Contents

Introduction

Swimming, sandcastling, surfing, scenery, watersports, fishing, wildlife watching or just lazing in the sun, Dorset's beaches have so much to offer. This practical guide is packed with key information, including parking, access and lifeguard cover, as well as facilities such as beach cafés, shops and toilets, to help you choose from over 50 Dorset beaches and coves dotted along 140km (88 miles) of remarkably varied coastal beauty. Each beach is illustrated.

Seashore Code

- Please help protect Dorset's wonderful coasts.
- Take litter home.
- Return all live specimens – crabs, prawns etc – to the water.
- Replace seaweeds and rocks where you find them.
- Report anything unusual.

Parking

For each beach there are grid references given for the car parks, sometimes more than one. Additionally the nearest post code is given for those who wish to use a SatNav. Parking charges vary and may change without notice.

Left: Lulworth Cove

Tourist Information Centres

Bournemouth 0845 051 1701
Blandford 01258 454770
Bridport 01308 424901
Christchurch 01202 471780
Dorchester 01305 267992
Lyme Regis 01297 442138
Poole 01202 253253
Portland 01305 861233
Shaftesbury 01747 853514
Sherborne 01935 815341
Swanage 01929 422885
Wareham 01929 552740
Weymouth 01305 785747
Wimborne 01202 886116

Although every effort was made to ensure the information given in this guide was accurate when we went to press, changes which are beyond our control can occur – another rock fall, for instance, or a change in lifeguard cover or dog regulations. If you encounter any problems, please tell us via our website: www.inspiringplaces.co.uk

Key to symbols used

Parking	Beware unstable cliffs	Café
Lifeguards (seasonal)	Sandy beach	Pub or bar
Disabled access	Good for swimming	Shops
Information point	Watersports	Sailing/boating
First aid	Beach huts	Fishing
Dogs allowed	Toilets	

Dogs banned (or seasonal restrictions)

Beach Safety

Dorset's beaches are delightful and safe – provided visitors take a few simple commonsense precautions and make safety their responsibility, especially with children. All beaches are affected by tides and currents, but some much more than others. Please check tide times, heed warning notices and keep well within the limits of your strength and skill.

Avoid swimming or boating alone or in rough seas. Observe posted warnings of dangerous currents. Do not swim if the red flag is flying or in zones covered by the black and white flag (watercraft only). On lifeguarded beaches, swim between the red/yellow flags. Some beaches have first aid facilities, telephones or lifeguard cover as shown in this book. In emergency, call the Coastguard on 999.

Being cut off by the rising tide is one of several potential hazards that can readily be avoided. Others include drifting out to sea on inflatable boats (never use them if the orange windsock is flying, it indicates offshore winds); slipping on wet rocks (wear shoes) and tunnelling deeply into soft sand, which can collapse. On certain beaches rock falls under unstable cliffs are a potential hazard. Please heed warning notices. Equally, keep away from cliff edges if exploring the Coast Path.

Disabled Access

Most beaches have disabled access and toilets that have disabled facilities. However some, such as Durdle Door, have steep steps or paths. Beaches with car parks very close by include Kimmeridge, Lulworth, Swanage, Avon Beach, Mudeford, Lyme Regis, Charmouth, Burton Bradstock, Ringstead Bay, Eype Mouth and Studland. Studland, Poole and Bournemouth beaches cater particularly well for disabled visitors.

Dogs

Where there are restrictions they generally apply to summer months. Great places for dog walking include Osmington Mills, Ringstead Bay and Lulworth.

Not all Dorset's beaches are accessible! But even so they can be enjoyed from the South West Coast Path, originally created to combat smugglers. The picture shows the coast west of Bat's Head. The nearest accessible beach is by Durdle Door.

Lyme Regis to Portland

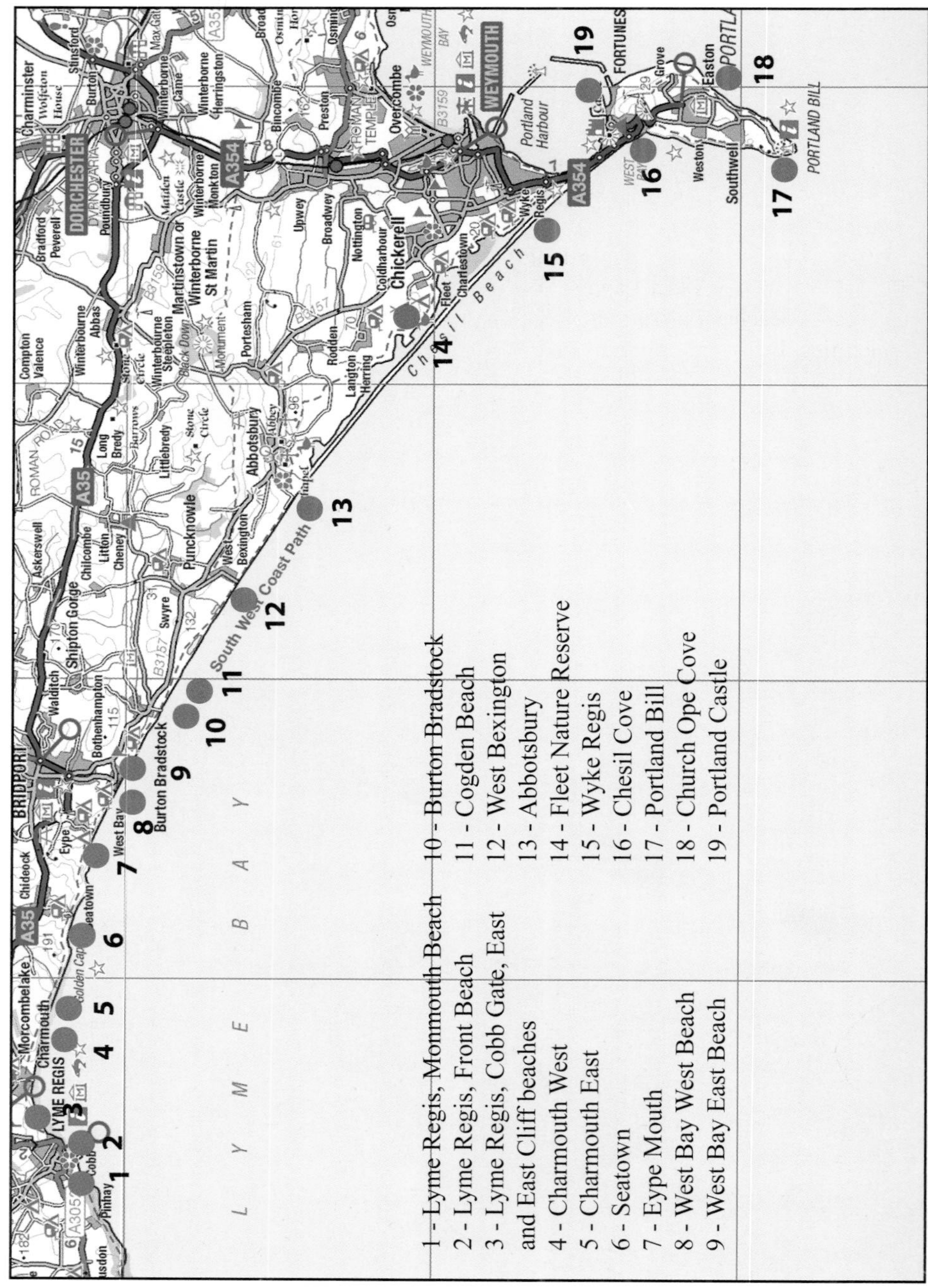

Between Lyme Regis and Burton Bradstock, West Dorset's beaches are predominantly shingle, with some sand at low tide and popular with families. Backed by impressive cliffs, including Golden Cap (191m/630ft) the highest Dorset cliff, this ruggedly beautiful part of the Jurassic Coast is famous for its remarkably rich fossil heritage. Fossil collecting draws many visitors year round, especially at Charmouth and Lyme Regis, which has a unique place in the development of scientific knowledge (page 10). Like West Bay, Lyme is a harbour town of character and history drawing numbers of visitors. Seatown and Eype Mouth offer quieter beaches of equal but different charm.

Chesil Bank stretches 29km (18 miles) south and east from Burton Bradstock to Portland Bill, a long and remarkable barrier beach sheltering the wildlife haven of Fleet Lagoon. However, I have treated access points with car parks as beaches in their own right, as they vary considerably in character and facilities, but share common characteristics. All are shingle, with ample space, especially at low tide. Great for beach fishing, they offer some scope for boating and swimming, but please heed warnings of strong tides and steep shelves and of rock falls along the westerly beaches.

Below, clockwise from top left: The west Dorset coast is a major fossil collecting area (photo courtesy of Lyme Regis Fossil Shop). A fishing boat in the harbour at Lyme Regis. The rocky shore at Osmington Mills and the promenade at Lyme Regis.

Lyme Regis - Front Beach

Family friendly and well sheltered by the Cobb, Lyme's Front Beach has fine sand and shallow water for children to play in. Like the neighbouring beaches, Cobb Gate and Monmouth, it's close to Lyme's many facilities and access is easy from the Cobb car park, with alternative parking a ten minute hike uphill at (the much cheaper) Holmbush car park.

The Cobb, a breakwater dating from the 14th century, makes a classic stroll – as readers of *Persuasion* and *The French Lieutenant's Woman* know. Enjoy the views and take a fishing trip or cruise from the pretty harbour, where pleasure craft and trawlers mingle. Visit the Lifeboat Station (01297 442230) with its viewing gallery and the aquarium (01297 444230), which houses local species of fish and shellfish.

(TIC)

SY337916, DT7 3JN
or SY337920, DT7 3JW
(both beaches)

Lyme Regis - Monmouth Beach

Monmouth Beach stretches over a kilometre west of Lyme's great breakwater, the Cobb. Pebbles predominate at high tide, with sand exposed at low tide. The beach is close to Lyme's many facilities and access is easy from the Cobb car park. Although this fills quickly in peak season, there's alternative parking a ten minute hike uphill at (the much cheaper) Holmbush car park.

Monmouth Beach is a great place for fossils: you may collect loose material, but digging and hammering are banned. Please leave larger ammonites for others to see on this SSSI. As with neighbouring beaches, avoid coming close to the cliffs because of the danger of rock falls and being cut off by the tide.

This beach was where the Duke of Monmouth, posing as the Protestant champion, landed in 1685 in his vain attempt to wrest the crown from his Catholic uncle, King James II. After defeat at the Battle of Sedgemoor, many of Monmouth's supporters were condemned to transportation or death. Twelve local men were hanged on Monmouth Beach.

Lyme Regis - Cobb Gate Beach SY343921, DT7 3QP or SY344926, DT7 3DR (main)

Backed by Marine Parade with its attractive medley of buildings, Cobb Gate Beach is a pebble bank at high tide, but offers sand at low tide – the best time to visit all Lyme's beaches. Family friendly like neighbouring Front Beach, it too enjoys easy access to Lyme's facilities, although parking at Cobb Gate itself is very limited.

Lyme Regis - East Cliff Beach and East Beach (as above)

East Cliff Beach is a small beach sandwiched between the much larger and rockier East Beach and Cobb Gate Beach. Really an easterly extension of Cobb Gate, it is again a mix of pebbles and sand. Dogs are permitted.

East Beach is a short walk from Lyme's facilities. Follow Marine Parade east from Cobb Gate. A mix of pebbles, sand and rock shelves, it is good for rockpooling at low tide – the best and only sensible time to visit, as the cliffs behind East Beach form the Black Ven landslide complex. Much studied by geologists, this landslide complex is active and there was a major landslide in 2008. Please heed warning notices and keep well clear of the cliffs, where the ever present danger of rock falls is compounded by the dangers of being cut off by the tide and stuck in deep mud.

Mary Anning and fossil collecting

Science owes much to the dedicated collecting of Lyme born fossil hunter Mary Anning (1799-1847), who directly found or pointed the way to nearly every specimen of importance in palaeontology according to science historian Stephen Jay Gould. Mary's work was largely done in winter, when landslips around Lyme reveal new fossils. Working quickly, she gathered her finds before the sea could claim them and thankfully survived the landslip that killed her dog in 1833. Despite her gender, humble background and modest education, her discoveries, including the first ichthyosaur to be correctly identified and the first two plesiosaur skeletons ever found, gained the attention of Henry Thomas De la Beche and William Buckland, two leading geologists of the time. She thus contributed to fundamental changes in scientific thinking, especially about the Earth's age, origins and development.

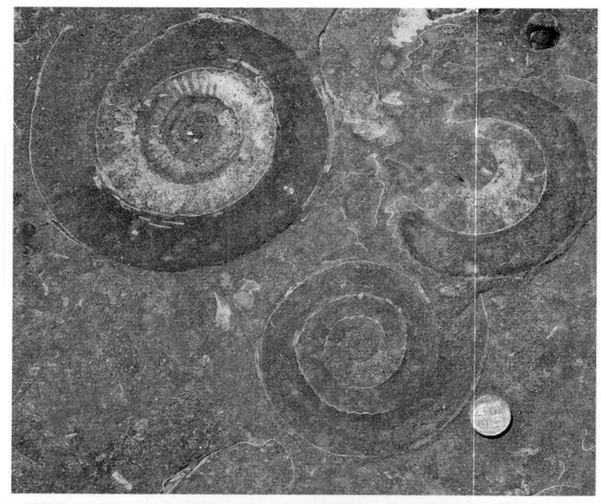

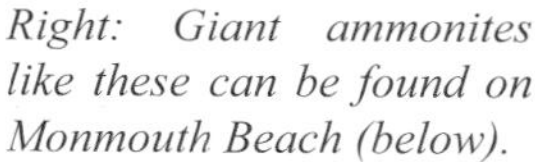

Right: Giant ammonites like these can be found on Monmouth Beach (below).

Charmouth - east and west SY365931, DT6 6QX

The two halves of Charmouth's long beach are divided by the River Char, but this is bridged at the beach. Similar in character, with great views along the Jurassic Coast, the upper areas of both beaches are pebbly, but low tide reveals more sand, especially on the eastern beach, making it the more popular. Both beaches are family friendly and suitable for a range of watersports including fishing, kayaking, boating and (in winter) surfing.

A car park lies between the two beaches, making access easy. The car park also has a café and shop, plus the Charmouth Heritage Coast Centre, where local fossils and geology are explained through interactive computers, colourful tableaux and children's activities. The Centre also has a good collection of local interest books and gifts for sale. The staff are helpful and friendly. From April to September, they offer a programme of fossil hunting trips and rockpool rambles. (Book on 01297 560772 or www.charmouth.org)

Indeed, fossil collecting is popular at Charmouth, especially along the western beach. Look along the foreshore, especially the area about 200m from the river mouth. Loose fossils may be gathered from the beach, but removing them from the cliffs by any means, including hammering, is forbidden. Please keep clear of the cliffs, they are unstable. Rock falls are a persistent danger throughout the year, and it is easy to become stuck in the mudslips. Dogs are allowed on Charmouth beaches in winter. In summer, they are banned from the western beach from May to September. They are also banned from the eastern beach, daytime from June to August.

Literary Lyme

Lyme Regis is connected with novelists Jane Austen and John Fowles. John Fowles (1926-2005) lived the second half of his life in Lyme Regis and set *The French Lieutenant's Woman,* his best known novel, in and around the town. The film version starred Meryl Streep as Sarah Woodruff and Jeremy Irons as Charles Smithson, who becomes obsessed by the enigmatic Sarah after seeing her staring out to sea from the Cobb. The remote farm at Underhill, Fowles' first home near Lyme, features as the dairy in the story.

Jane Austen visited Lyme in 1803 and 1804 and placed much of her last novel, *Persuasion,* here. In *Persuasion,* the Cobb also plays a crucial role after Louisa Musgrove falls from it. Anne Elliot, the heroine, begins to win back the admiration of Captain Wentworth (hero) by administering first aid to the injured girl. See www.literarylyme.co.uk for literary walking tours of Lyme.

Seatown SY421918, DT6 6JU

Seatown's ample shingle beach stretches 2km between Ridge Cliff and the highest and most impressive cliff on the Dorset coast, Golden Cap (191m/630ft). Once the narrow lane from Chideock has been negotiated, access is very easy: the Anchor Inn, plus a café, shop, telephone and toilets are all right by the beachside car park. There's space aplenty for beach fishing or staking your little kingdom by the sea. Low tide is good for ammonite fossil hunting on the foreshore year round. Swimming is possible, but please heed warnings of tides and currents and keep clear of the cliffs.

Eype Mouth SY448911, DT6 6AL

Eype Mouth is a long, predominantly pebble beach, with superb views over Lyme Bay and the dramatic cliffs of the Jurassic Coast both east and west. Reached via a long, narrow lane through the attractive village of Lower Eype with its pub and hotel, the beach is refreshingly simple and uncommercialized. Access from the car park is short and easy, so long as you can manage the steps.

West Bay SY465905, DT6 4GD (both beaches and harbour)

With a good range of facilities, spectacular coastal views and two long beaches separated by a pretty harbour bustling with fishing boats and leisure craft, West Bay is popular with families. There is plenty to do from swimming (beware strong currents and steep shelf) to beach fishing, or an old fashioned stroll around the harbour and esplanade for ice cream or fish and chips. West Bay also has a swimming pool, amusement arcades, play areas and a leisure complex. Boatmen offer fishing trips and coastal cruises, or you can hire a rowing boat.

West Beach

Slightly further from the many facilities of West Bay, the West Beach enjoys good access and parking. A long beach of pebbles with some sand at low tide, West Beach is continuous with the beach at Eype Mouth when the tide is out.

East Beach

Backed by beautiful golden sandstone cliffs, East Beach has coarse sand and small pebbles and plenty of space to stake your kingdom in the sun. At low tide it is continuous with beaches further east. Like West Beach, it benefits from easy access and convenient parking.

West Bay Harbour

The harbour at West Bay is not natural but has been created by cutting a channel through the beach and excavating a hollow behind it. The present one dates from the 1740s but a harbour has existed here for hundreds of years, built for the export of rope produced in nearby Bridport.

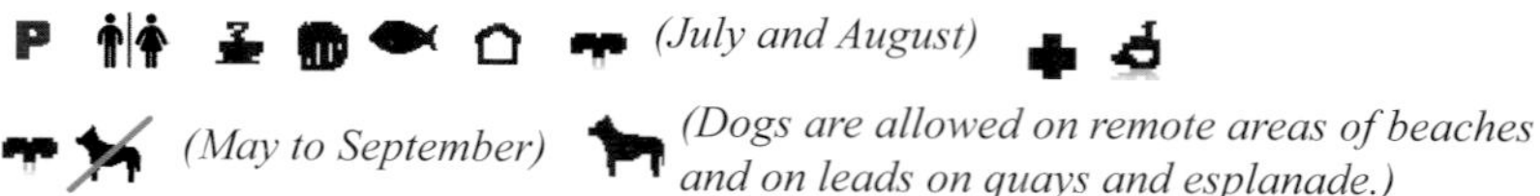

Burton Bradstock SY492888, DT6 4RG

Easily accessed from the beachside National Trust car park, Hive Beach is a long stretch of steeply shelving shingle, offering visitors a good deal of space even at the height of summer. Beach fishing is popular, as is fossil hunting, boating, kayaking and sailboarding – but please heed posted warnings of the strong tides and undertow if swimming or going on the water. The large café and toilets are well sited right by the beach, which is overlooked by a Coastwatch station.

(June to September)

Cogden Beach SY502886, DT6 4RL

Cogden is a continuation of neighbouring Hive Beach and similar in character, with its steeply shelved shingle. However, it has no facilities of its own and thus attracts fewer visitors. There's ample space, making it ideal for a quiet family day out, fishing, or exercising dogs. As usual with beaches along this coast, visitors are warned of strong tides and currents. A 500m long path slopes gently down to Cogden from the National Trust car park, passing through herb rich maritime grassland. This is grazed by cattle and maintained without chemical fertilizers to encourage a rich variety of flowering plants, including sea kale, thrift and yellow-horned poppy. Butterflies are plentiful. Look out too for birds, including linnets, skylarks, warblers and buntings – plus wildfowl like gadwall and wigeon in winter. Sea birds often seen include various gulls, cormorants, guillemots, razorbills and common terns.

West Bexington SY531865, DT2 9DG

Another Chesil shingle beach, West Bexington benefits from a beachside car park and handy café, shop, pub and toilets. As is the case with other Chesil beaches, swimmers should beware of the steep shelf, as well as waves and tides. Beach fishing can yield a varied catch. Species caught include mackerel, garfish, bass and plaice, plus cod, whiting and dogfish in winter. Behind the beach is a Nature Reserve. With a mix of habitats - reed bed, scrub and wet meadow – it shelters a variety of flora and fauna.

(but rough terrain)

Abbotsbury Beach and attractions SY560846, DT3 4LA

Abbotsbury's spacious shingle beach is easily accessed from the car park, which has its own café and toilets. It has a markedly steeper shelf than the Chesil beaches further west. Like them, it is popular with fishermen.

Abbotsbury is an exceptionally attractive stone built village with cafés, shops and pubs, plus three notable tourist attractions. The Sub-Tropical Gardens (01305 871387 www.abbotsburygardens.co.uk), has 20 acres of rare plants from around the world and deserves considerable time to explore thoroughly. Abbotsbury Swannery, the oldest managed swan population in the world, has up to 600 birds (admission charge, details www.abbotsburyswannery.co.uk 01305 871858). Feeding times are especially interesting, as they are at Abbotsbury's Children's Farm (01305 871817 www.abbotsburychildrensfarm.co.uk), where there are pony rides, bottle feeding lambs, milking the cow and much besides.

*Please observe access restrictions the Fleet end of the beach.

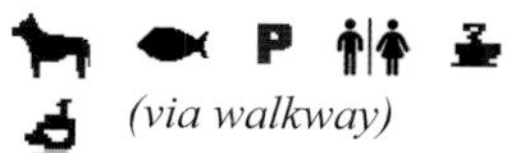

(via walkway)

In Search of Moonfleet

John Meade Falkner based his perennially popular smuggling novel Moonfleet (1898) on East Fleet, a hamlet on the Fleet Lagoon. Place plays a large part in the story and many locations along the Dorset coast can readily be identified, although some descriptions have been embroidered and others have thinly disguised fictional names such as Monkbury for Abbotsbury. Park at East Fleet's new church and collect a leaflet 'Discovering Moonfleet' in the porch. Walk back 500m along the lane and turn right down Butter Street to visit Moonfleet's old church, with its memorials to Meade Falkner and the Mohun family. The nave of the church and much of the village was destroyed in 1824 when a great storm breached Chesil Bank. This may have been Meade Falkner's inspiration for the storm in which Elzivir Block loses his life saving John Trenchard in the story. A short walk over the footbridge and left to the (normally tranquil) Fleet Lagoon gives beautiful views and good birdwatching.

The old church at East Fleet.

The Fleet Nature Reserve

An exceptional barrier beach, the longest in Britain, Chesil Bank is 29km long, 200m wide and comprises 100 million tons of pebbles. These vary from pea size at West Bay to the size of oranges at Portland. It is said local sailors knew where they had landed simply by the size of the beach pebbles.

Chesil Bank rises in height and steepness towards its south-eastern end, reaching 15m at Portland. Behind it lies the Fleet Lagoon, a rich wildlife reserve supporting fresh, brackish and salt water species of plants and flocks of birds.

One way to see the Fleet Lagoon and its birds is to visit Abbotsbury Swannery (page 13). Alternatively, explore the South West Coast Path between Langton Herring and Ferry Bridge near Wyke Regis, where there is a visitor centre with birdwatchers' telescopes for public use (page 18). Another good access point which involves only 2km walking is East Fleet, the fictional Moonfleet of John Meade Falkner's smuggling novel.

The Fleet at Rodden Hive.

Wyke Regis SY668756, DT4 9XE

A short scrunch up and over the 15m high bank of pebbles from Ferry Bridge car park and visitor centre gives access to the southern end of Chesil Beach. Like neighbouring Chesil beaches, this one is popular with fishermen. Dogs are permitted, but please keep them away from the Fleet Lagoon, especially the bird breeding area and the mudflats. Effectively a glass fronted hide, the visitor centre has telescopes for public use and underwater and terrestrial cameras for visitors to watch fish and nesting birds. There is information on Chesil Beach, quarrying on Portland and the Fleet and Chesil Beach Nature Reserve, with its internationally important colony of Little Terns. Enquire for guided walks around the reserve and for trips in the Fleet Observer, a glass bottomed boat.

Windsurfers off Portland

Chesil Cove on Portland SY684734, DT5 1AP

A long curving beach of large pebbles at the southern end of Chesil Bank, Chesil Cove is especially popular with fishermen, divers and snorkelers, who appreciate its clear water and marine life. However, being on the exposed western side of Portland, Chesil Cove has a steep shelf and can be subject to strong tides and currents - as many ships have discovered to their cost. Other features of Chesil Cove include easy access and free parking as signed on Brandy Row. The Cove has a pleasant promenade, with a café terrace overlooking at one end and a pub garden the other; an imaginative public sculpture The Chesil Earthworks and an abundance of wildlife, especially lime loving plants and butterflies.

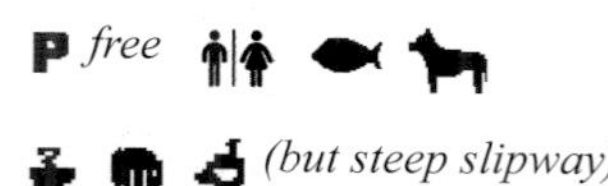

Portland Bill Lighthouse

Portland Bill's 41m tall lighthouse is regularly open to the public. Climbing the 153 steps is rewarded with splendid coastal views. There has been a lighthouse on Portland since 1716 when two towers with enclosed lanterns and coal fires were constructed by Trinity House to guide vessels heading for Portland and Weymouth through the Portland Race, and to act as a waymark for mariners navigating the English Channel. The current tower dates from 1906. It was automated in 1996 and is now monitored from Trinity House's operational HQ in Harwich by telemetric link. More information: www.trinityhouse.co.uk.

(Photograph courtesy of Trinity House.)

Portland Castle

One of the best preserved coastal forts ordered by King Henry VIII to deter French attack; Portland Castle was built solidly of stone ashlar in 1539-40 and is very well preserved. Visitors can explore the gun platforms with their canon, the garrison's quarters, Captain's House and Heritage Garden with an audio tour explaining the castle's original role in deterring French and Spanish aggression and later service in the First and Second World Wars. Features include a Second World War display, weaponry, Tudor kitchen, explanatory plaques and children's activity room. For events programme and details see www.english-heritage.org.uk phone 01305 820539.

Church Ope Cove on Portland SY695712, DT5 1HT

Church Ope Cove is a small beach of pebbles and rocks with some sand. A shallower shelf than the Chesil Bank beaches make Church Ope a good family beach and swimming is safe within the cove. Diving and snorkeling are popular in the clear water. It's also well sheltered from westerly winds by Portland itself and a ring of low cliffs. Parking is free, but shared with Portland Museum, so spaces are in short supply at busy times. Access is via a moderately steep path with steps, leading past the ruins of the 13th century church which gives this pleasant cove its name.

P *free*

Weymouth to Poole

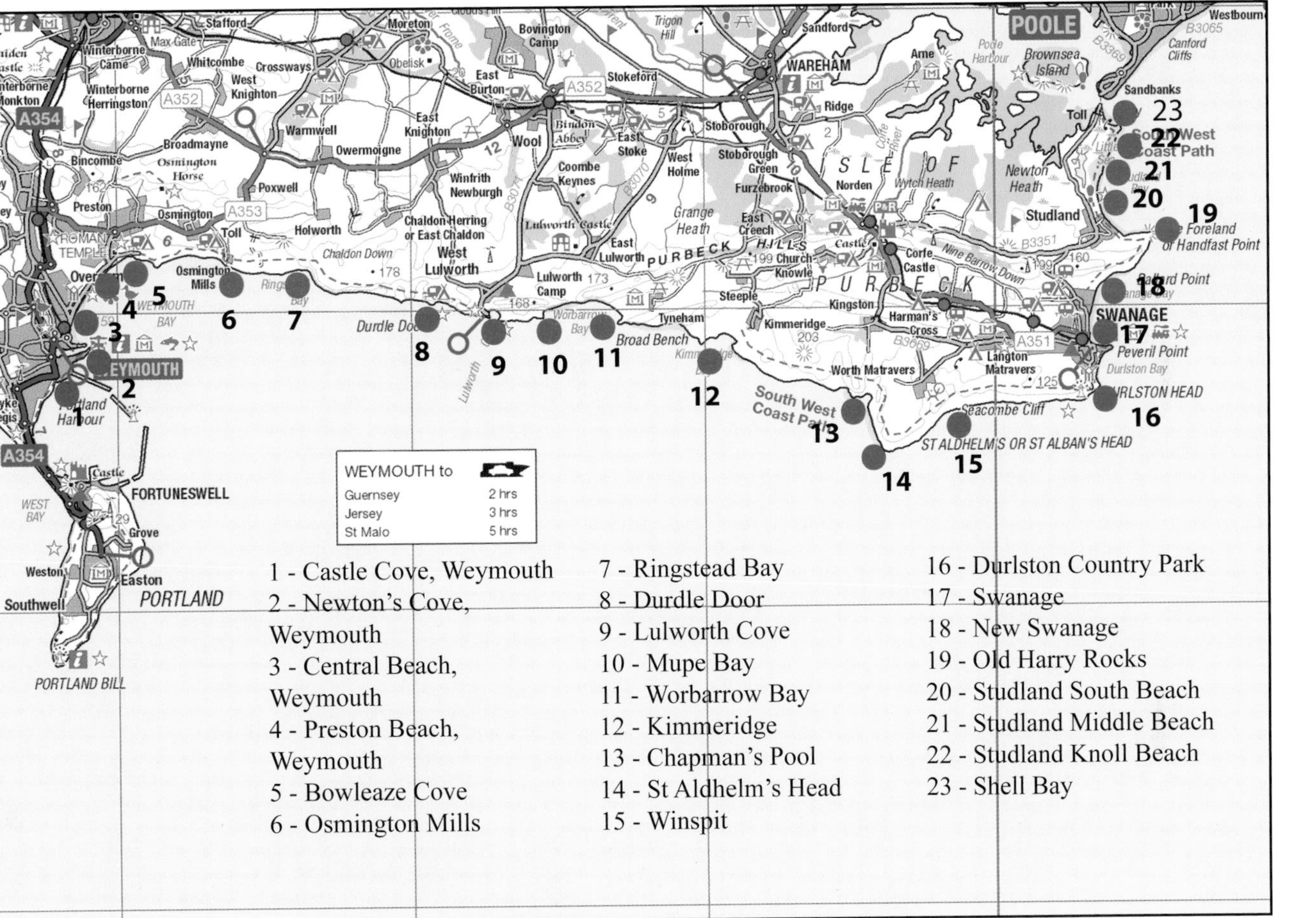

Sheltered from westerly winds by Portland, Weymouth Bay has a quite different character to West Dorset. Its long beaches of golden sand washed by gentle waves are ideal for family holidays. Deck chairs, donkey rides, Punch and Judy shows, beach huts, merry-go-rounds and pedal boats, Weymouth epitomizes the English seaside resort and has one of England's most handsome seafronts.

Protected by Purbeck, the east facing bays of Swanage and Studland enjoy a similarly benign character. The ideal places to build a sandcastle or take a dip in the briny, their lovely sandy beaches have been deservedly popular for generations. Equally, they are perfect for a variety of watersports, especially sailing and kayaking, whilst their clear waters are well suited to snorkeling and diving.

Between Weymouth Bay and Durlston Head the beaches are mainly pebbles and rock. Most visited are Durdle Door, its iconic limestone arch separating two splendid beaches, and Lulworth Cove, its great circle of folded rocks a book on the geological past. Whilst Ringstead, Kimmeridge and Osmington are family beaches, remote Chapman's Pool and Winspit are harder to access and less visited, as are Mupe Bay and Worbarrow Bay, where access is also restricted by the Army. However, if you're looking for tranquility and natural beauty, the effort is well worthwhile.

Exploring Weymouth's Esplanade and Harbour

Weymouth is a seaside resort of character with a rich heritage of historic buildings. The Esplanade, with its long Georgian terraces, makes one of England's finest seafronts. Packed with fishing boats and yachts, the harbour is full of interest, with a pleasant jumble of 19th century buildings, ships chandlers, pubs and cafés. Follow the signs from the southern end of the Esplanade, take the rowing boat ferry to the far shore, turn right and re-cross by the lifting bridge. Make your way back to the Esplanade via a maze of old streets and take a stroll along the seafront. You'll be in royal company: King George III popularized Weymouth and gave his patronage to the then novel idea of sea bathing. His statue stands by the Esplanade, not far from the splendid clock tower celebrating Victoria's 1887 Jubilee.

Castle Cove, Weymouth SY676776, DT4 8QG

A very small beach of fine golden sand, Castle Cove enjoys a pretty outlook across Portland Harbour and eastwards to the high Purbeck cliffs. Well protected by the Breakwater, its shallow water is perfect for children. Car access is via the Old Castle Road from the A354, with parking right by the cove. However, parking spaces are limited. Note that public access to Castle Cove is by agreement with Castle Cove Sailing Club, so please observe notices about parking, removing litter and preventing dogs from fouling the beach.

Newton's Cove, Weymouth SY680783, DT4 8UT

This small cove is a mix of pebbles, rocks and coarse sand. It has a pleasant promenade lined with benches and attractive views eastwards to the Purbeck cliffs. Drivers should follow signs from the A379 for Old Nothe Fort and park in Weymouth's Old Town (East) car park. A short level walk and a flight of steps leads to Newton's Cove, which has no facilities of its own, but is fairly close to those of Weymouth. A plaque by the promenade commemorates the men and women of Allied Coastal Forces who served in HMS Bee between 1941-45. From here, Motor Torpedo Boats, Motor Gun Boats and Motor Launches attacked enemy shipping.

Weymouth's Central Beach SY678792, DT4 8NA (one possibility)

With its long sweep of fine golden sand backed by handsome Georgian and Victorian terraces and magnificent views of the Jurassic Coast, Weymouth's seafront is one of the most impressive in England. As you would expect of a leading family resort, it is well managed with a wide range of facilities, including deckchairs, beach huts, pedalos, amusement arcades, Punch and Judy shows, tram rides, boat trips, trampolines and crazygolf. The gently shelving lifeguarded beach is ideal for sandcastling, paddling and swimming. Canoeing and snorkeling are popular too. With so much to offer, Weymouth attracts a lot of visitors, especially in season. On street parking may be scarce, the one way system isn't easy to negotiate and drivers usually choose between the town car parks or the park and ride service. Once at the seafront, access to the beach is easy via ramps. The town has a programme of special events from the International Beach Kite Festival to fireworks, chase the Christmas pudding and more. Call Tourist Information for current details.

Below left: Weymouth's main beach has all the traditional family attractions! Below right: Weymouth's famous Regency esplanade.

Dog area at south end.

(TIC at Pavilion)

Preston Beach, Weymouth SY688808, DT4 7SX (Lodmoor Country Park)

Preston and Overcombe Beach lies between Greenhill Beach and Bowleaze Cove. With its sand and shingle it is similar in character to Greenhill. It has good parking and access and there is ample room for varied activities, with designated areas for bathing, ski-boating and sailboarding. At the Greenhill end is a children's paddling pool, Greenhill Gardens and Lodmoor Country Park, with its nature reserve, sea life park, pitch and putt, miniature railway and other attractions.

(Greenhill)

Bowleaze Cove SY696816 DT3 6PU (south), SY703820, DT3 6PW (north)

The northern end of Weymouth Bay, Bowleaze Cove is family friendly and continuous with Preston and Overcombe Beach. Most people use the sandier northern end of the cove, which has a large car park, good access, restaurant, fun fair, shop and WC, plus designated areas for bathing and jet ski-ing. The southern (Preston) end of this long beach has more shingle, but is usually quieter. It has its own car park, beach shop and café. Again, access is good, though some visitors park on the road between the two ends of the beach and walk.

P

Osmington Mills SY735816, DT3 6HF

A predominantly rocky beach with some gravel, sand and rock pools, Osmington Mills beach calls for some modest agility. It is accessed via a short walk. Either take the stepped path behind the conveniently sited Smuggler's Inn, or use the steeper and rougher path from the end of the pub car park. There is also on road parking, but this is sometimes all taken in high season.

P

Right: The Smuggler's Inn at Osmington Mills is very popular. It was once the base of a famous smuggler known as "French Peter".

Ringstead Bay SY752814, DT2 8NG

A well sheltered beach of large pebbles with some sand and rock pools, Ringstead's shallow water makes it ideal for children and family boating, but jet skis are not permitted. The car park, café and shop are all close and the beach is easily accessed.

Durdle Door SY812805, BH20 5PU

Durdle Door Beach and Man of War Bay are two long neighbouring shingle beaches separated by the famous limestone arch, Durdle Door. They are both accessed by steep, stepped paths from the cliff top car park on the far side of the caravan site, where there is a café, telephones and shops. A mobile snack bar is parked by the path down to the beaches in season. The natural beauty of Durdle Door and its spectacular cliffs attract numbers of visitors. Bathing is possible, but beware the steep shelf.

Right: Man O'War Bay with its long, sheltered beach. Bathing is safer here. Below: Durdle Door.

Lulworth Cove SY823800, BH20 5RH

Sheltered by spectacularly folded rocks, Lulworth Cove is a near perfect circle of wonderfully clear water. This makes it ideal for boating and swimming, though it shelves quite steeply. The beach is predominantly pebbles with some sand and is easily accessed from Lulworth's large car park or by a ten minute walk from (limited) roadside parking near the church. At high tide the eastern end of the beach is only accessible by the steep, stepped Coast Path, but it is well worth seeing. Beyond, the Coast Path leads to the Fossil Forest (page 29) and Mupe Bay. However, the land east of Lulworth belongs to the MOD and is only open to the public on certain weekends, most public holidays and most of August. (Always check before visiting 01929 404819 to avoid disappointment). Lulworth is well provided with shops, cafés and pubs whilst its Heritage Centre (free entry) offers a film describing the area's world famous geology, as well as excellent displays of local fossils and rocks; history; archaeology and natural history. Boat and kayak tours from Lulworth provide another way of seeing the Jurassic Coast.

P *(but ramp is quite steep)*

Mupe Bay (Parking, facilities and access restrictions as above)

Although Mupe Bay is a large beach of coarse sand and shingle surrounded by high and dramatic cliffs, it is less visited than most beaches - you may well have it to yourself out of season. Reaching it calls for a 2.5km (1½ mile) walk from Lulworth Cove, where all the facilities noted above are located. At low tide, you may walk around the Lulworth Cove beach and then follow the fairly level Range Walk, but at the top of the tide walkers must climb the steep cliff path above the cove before joining the Range Walk. Either way, there are superb views of the cove and the coastline east and west.

Worbarrow Bay SY882803, BH20 5DE

Worbarrow Bay is a long beach of shingle with some sand at lower reaches of the tide. Backed by high and dramatic cliffs, it's a great place to explore, admire the views or walk a dog, but please stick to footpaths and beware rock falls. Access is via a gentle 20 minute walk from Tyneham (page 29), where there is a car park and toilets. Like Tyneham, Worbarrow is part of the Army ranges and access is limited (page 27). Noted for its abundant wildlife, especially woodland and downland birds, Worbarrow is also a magnet for geologists. As well as the impressive chalk cliffs to the west, the strangely shaped headland at the eastern end of Worbarrow Bay called Worbarrow Tout and adjoining Pondfield Cove are textbook examples of cliffs folded by massive tectonic forces as the African and European continents collided some 30 million years ago. Remorseless pounding by the sea has carved out both Worbarrow Bay and Pondfield Cove, as well as creating sea caves. Dinosaur footprints have also been found at Worbarrow Tout.

Pondfield Cove

Pondfield Cove is easily overlooked by visitors to Worbarrow Bay. Tucked in between folded limestone cliffs of Gold Down and the western side of Worbarrow Tout, this rocky cove has a beauty of its own.

The Fossil Forest

The remarkable Fossil Forest is just inside the Range east of Lulworth Cove. Whilst there are reasonably good views of the fossils from the path, a close view means turning right near the gate and following steps down to a rocky ledge. What we see are not the trees themselves, but the fossilized remains of the algal burrs that grew around massive cypress and monkey-puzzle trees which thrived for a period after sea levels dropped in the late Jurassic. The sea rose again, killing the trees with salt water. Accumulated mud stuck to the algae and hardened into limestone rings.

Above: Fossilised algal growth around the hole left by the stump of a Jurassic tree. In the bottom picture the trees were lying horizontally.

Tyneham

The deserted village of Tyneham is a time capsule with its own poignant story. Along with the downland and coast between Lulworth and Kimmeridge, Tyneham was requisitioned by the Army and evacuated in 1943 to allow troops to train for the D Day landings in Normandy. Although the villagers were promised they could return after the Second World War was won, permission was refused. Tyneham and surrounding area remain under MOD control and public access is limited to the same periods as Mupe Bay, Worbarrow and the Fossil Forest.

Tyneham church has been preserved with tableaux showing period photographs and memories of villagers and village life in the late nineteenth and early twentieth centuries. Also preserved is the schoolhouse. Children's names mark the clothes pegs in the lobby. Old fashioned teaching aids hang on the classroom walls and samples of the children's work lie on the bench desks. It seems the school bell only rang an hour ago.

Ruined and roofless cottages too have tableaux telling the histories of the families who lived in them, along with photographs of them at work and play. Although the farmhouse has gone, Tyneham Farm remains, its hand tools, stables, horse drawn harrow and farm wagon a reminder of the recent past when men and horses rather than tractors and diesel machinery provided motive power.

Kimmeridge SY908791, BH20 5PF

A sizeable beach of rocky ledges, pebbles and coarse sand, Kimmeridge is close to its car park at the end of the toll road. There is a farm shop and licensed café a mile away in the village and an ice cream van visits the beach. Fossil hunting is popular at Kimmeridge; but please keep clear of the unstable cliffs – there are good opportunities for finding fossils along the foreshore and low tide also reveals interesting rock pools. Find out more about local marine life at the Marine Centre (free entry) at the western end of the beach. The centre has a live aquaria and displays of marine flora and fauna. There are children's activities, details of marine events and a snorkeling trail, for which visitors can buy or hire masks and snorkels. (Details www.dorsetwildlifetrust.org.uk 01929 481044).

Chapman's Pool SY956787, BH20 5LN or SY954794, BH20 5LL (Kingston)

A large and largely deserted beach of sand and gravel beneath very high, impressive cliffs, Chapman's Pool is a place to escape the crowds and contemplate the scenery. It is ideal for walking the dog, fishing and looking for fossils, but please beware of the unstable cliffs and remember you may be on your own if you go swimming. Reaching this idyll requires some effort. Whilst it's possible to access Chapman's Pool via steep (and possibly slippery) footpaths from the car park near Worth Matravers, the better and less arduous route is to follow South Street out of Kingston. At the end of South Street, walk down the track to the beach – the last part of this mile long path is a bit steep and calls for some agility. There is very limited parking at the beach end of South Street, but if this is already taken you will have to park (with care) in Kingston village and walk the extra ¾ mile. Chapman's Pool has no facilities, but there is a pub and a phone in Kingston, plus a pub and toilets in Worth Matravers (page 32).

St. Aldhelm's Head SY964775, BH19 3LL (or as for Winspit)

St. Aldhelm's Head can be reached via the coast path from Winspit or from the car park on the west side of Worth Matravers (reference above). This rocky headland of Portland Stone commands wonderful views along the Jurassic Coast. The lovely Norman style chapel is worth a visit and there has probably been a place of worship on this spot long before the present one was built. It could well be that a church was founded here by Aldhelm, the first Bishop of Sherborne, in the 8th century.

Right: View from St. Aldhelm's Head

Winspit SY974777, BH19 3LE

Winspit is a beautiful cove of rocky ledges and boulders with good rockpooling. Facilities, including parking, are in Worth Matravers. The last part of the 20 minute walk from the village requires some nimble footwork. Whether visiting the cove or the nearby quarries, please heed warning notices and remember the rocks may be slippery and unstable. Worth Matravers is a most attractive village. Built of local stone, it is centred on its green and duck pond. The church is Norman and the historic pub, named the Square and Compass after the mason's symbolic tools, has an excellent museum of local fossils and archaeological finds.

Winspit has lots of rocky ledges for sitting and soaking up the sun. Look out for the giant ammonite fossil on the foreshore

Durlston Country Park SZ032773, BH19 1AP

Signed from Swanage, Durlston Country Park is 300 acres of sea cliffs, grassland and woodland managed for conservation. There are well designed woodland, cliff top and wildlife trails, with good paths and easy access. Get a trail leaflet from Durlston Castle Visitor Centre, which is open all year and has an interesting events programme, as well as displays of geology and wildlife, an art gallery and temporary exhibitions (www.durlston.co.uk). Live cameras are focused on birds and other wildlife. Indeed, Durlston Head is a great place to watch birds, especially sea birds, all year, but particularly during spring and autumn migrations. There is a bird hide and also a dolphin watch hut: April, May and December being the best months for spotting dolphins. Also of interest at Durlston are Anvil Point lighthouse and the Great Globe, a 40 ton limestone sphere of Portland Stone representing the Earth.

Swanage SZ026792, BH19 1AP

A traditional family seaside resort, Swanage has a huge beach of fine golden sand, with shallow water ideal for bathing and watersports. Canoes and pedal boats can be hired, as well as beach huts, deck chairs and sun loungers. There's plenty of entertainment, including crazy golf, bowls, a fun fair, amusement arcades and Punch and Judy shows. Swanage also benefits from its cinema/theatre, whilst the Museum and Heritage Centre has videos and displays on local history and wildlife. The handsome pier dates from 1897 and has a Victorian museum with period photos and posters; Victorian penny slot machines; history displays and a bathing machine. There is also a diving school located on the pier. As well as beach cafés, Swanage has a wide choice of pubs, cafés, restaurants, shops and accommodation. There are several car parks within moderate walking distance of the beach (accessed by ramps) and out of season parking on the long sea front. Alternatively, use the Norden park and ride near Corfe Castle and take the six mile long steam railway into Swanage.

May to Sept.

New Swanage SZ028798, BH19 1PJ

Continuous with Swanage main beach, New Swanage is equally family friendly, with golden sand and shallow water. It has its own WCs, café and shop. Beach huts, deck chairs, canoes, pedal boats and jet ski rides can all be hired at the Swanage end of the beach. Access is moderately easy from Swanage North car park and there is out of season parking on the sea front. Otherwise, find roadside parking in New Swanage and use the path *and steps* by the Grand Hotel. The beach is vast at low tide when it is possible to walk over the hard, wet sand for 1½ miles (2.5km) towards the white cliffs at Ballard Point. Low tide is definitely the best time to explore: as the tide rises you will be obliged to climb over the groynes and there is a danger of being cut off at high tide. Moreover, the red and yellow cliffs of Ballard Down are unstable. Please note that the promenade and beach huts at New Swanage are privately owned.

Studland

All four Studland beaches are managed by the National Trust. Popular and family friendly, they have fine golden sand and sheltered, shallow water suitable for bathing and watersports. Facilities are good and maintained to a high standard. There are designated picnic and barbeque areas and easy access from the car parks, which are free to NT members. Although similar, there are some significant differences between the Studland beaches, as described below.

Studland - South Beach SZ038825, BH19 3AL

Separated by the tide from Middle Beach, South Beach is a short walk from both the car park and the Bankes Arms. There is also a beach café. A popular 1 mile level walk along the Coast Path leads to Handfast Point and spectacular views of Old Harry Rocks.

P

Studland - Middle Beach SZ036829, BH19 3AX

Continuous with Knoll and Shell beaches, Middle Beach has a sizeable boat park as well as a handy car park. It is home of the Studland Sea School, which offers a wide range of sea kayaking, kayak fishing and sit on top courses, guiding, tours and hire for all levels of ability. Snorkeling and fishing equipment is also available (www.studlandseaschool.co.uk). A path over the low cliffs links Middle and South beaches. It passes Fort Henry, with its Second World War pill boxes, anti-tank devices and memorial: a reminder of the vital role played by Dorset in the preparations for and launch of the Normandy invasions in 1944.

Studland - Knoll Beach SZ034836, BH19 3AH

Knoll Beach too is easily accessible, family friendly and ideal for watersports. The hire shop offers pedal boats, waterbikes, kayaks, windsurfers, wetsuits, deckchairs, sunbeds and powerboat rides, whilst the visitor centre has informative exhibitions about Studland. At the north of Knoll Beach is a kite surfing area. Signs on the remoter part towards Shell Beach mark the area used by naturists.

P

Old Harry Rocks (as Studland South Beach)

The Old Harry Rocks at Handfast Point can be reached via an easy stroll from the National Trust car park at South Beach. Take great care with dogs as the cliffs are sheer. The Chalk here represents the end of the Jurassic Coast and was deposited in a shallow, tropical sea around 65 million years ago at the end of the Cretaceous Period. Following this came the great extinction when the dinosaurs, ammonites and many other species were wiped out, probably due to the inpact of a giant asteroid.

Studland - Shell Bay SZ035863, BH19 3BA

The northern end of Studland's 3 mile long sand beach, Shell Beach is backed by dunes supporting marram grass and heather. Please avoid trampling them as much as possible to protect them and the varied wildlife they support. Shell Beach is easily accessed from the NT car park, though some drivers use roadside parking and walk. On the north side of the Sandbanks Ferry road Bramble Bush Bay effectively forms a continuation of Shell Beach. A small, sandy beach, it overlooks Poole Harbour and is popular with fishermen.

Studland Heath National Nature Reserve (as Shell Bay)

Knoll Beach stretches north to join Shell Beach and behind both beaches is Studland and Godlingston Heath National Nature Reserve, 1541 acres (631ha) of sand dunes, heathland, scrub, woodland, bogs and fresh water supporting a wide variety of wildlife. Species of note include the Dartford warbler, sand lizard, smooth snake and nightjar. There are signed trails and wardens offer guided tours.

Poole to Christchurch

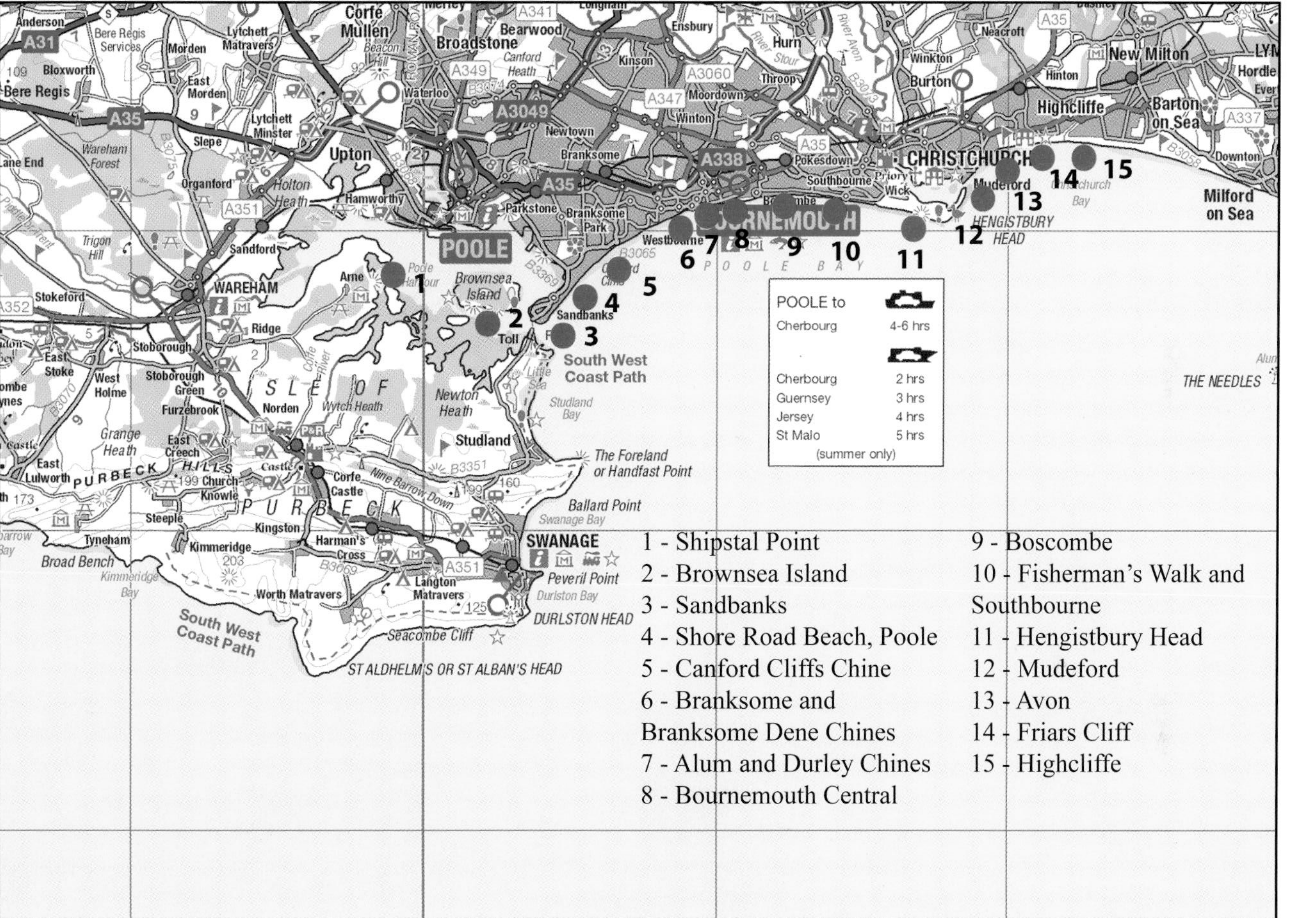

Poole Bay has some of Dorset's most popular family beaches – hardly surprising with more than 18km (11¼ miles) of continuous sandy beach stretching from the Sandbanks Ferry to Hengistbury Head east of Bournemouth. Beyond Christchurch Harbour, predominantly sandy beach again stretches eastwards from Mudeford Quay around Christchurch Bay to Highcliffe and on into Hampshire.

The beaches along Poole and Christchurch Bays are well managed with good, often excellent, facilities. Entry points and car parks are regularly spaced and the beaches sensibly zoned for swimming, watersports and exercising dogs. With extensive lifeguard cover, this attractive part of the Dorset coast is ideal for children, but is also suitable for a range of sports including kite surfing, surfing, sailing, windsurfing and kayaking.

Bournemouth particularly offers a plethora of additional entertainments from an aquarium, fun fairs, amusement arcades and theatres to deckchairs and strolls on the piers and promenade. Naturally, such a well established seaside resort has plenty of visitors, especially in season. For something more tranquil, visit Brownsea Island and Hengistbury Head, both noted for their natural beauty and wildlife.

Sandbanks Peninsular Beach SZ044877, BH13 7QD

The most westerly of the Poole and Bournemouth beaches - effectively one long beach stretching over 18km (11¼ miles) east to Hengistbury Head – Sandbanks is a long beach of fine golden sand with shallow water, ideal for families. Like other Poole and Bournemouth beaches, it is well managed and has good facilities, including outdoor showers, drinking water and a barbeque area. Access is direct from the car parks. Use the map by the beach office to get your bearings, find the crazy golf and road train and see the way the beach is zoned for various activities, including barbeques, fishing and watersports. Swimming is between the flags by the lifeguard station; dogs are confined to the southern end of the beach by the Sandbanks ferry.

P

Brownsea Island beaches SZ019892, BH15 1UY (Poole Quay) or as Sandbanks. It is often possible to park on roads near the Sandbanks ferry.

Beautifully situated in Poole Harbour, Brownsea has a great deal to offer and merits a full day's visit exploring on foot, enjoying the views and discovering the island's interesting history and richly varied wildlife. It has excellent facilities and is managed by the National Trust (entrance charge for non-members). Access is by passenger boats from Sandbanks or Poole Quay. Brownsea's attractive family friendly beach of sand and pebbles is good for paddling, swimming and picnics. It's a 20-30 minute walk from reception (ask for a map) via the excellent Visitor Centre. This has comprehensive displays and introductory films showing Brownsea as the birthplace of the Scout and Guide Movement and a haven for wildlife, notably red squirrels, sika deer and many sea birds and waders. From the Visitor Centre, walk ahead to the viewpoint and follow steps down to the beach or continue towards South Shore Lodge, where a gentler track leads down to the shore. Note except for assistance dogs, dogs are banned from the island. Information: boats 01929 462383; National Trust 01202 707744.

Brownsea's beach offers peace and quiet for those willing to walk a little. The island has many other attractive locations; below left the church and right Brownsea Castle.

Shipstal Point, Poole Harbour SY973878, BH20 5BJ (Shipstal Point is about a 2km walk from the RSPB car park)

The RSPB Nature Reserve at Arne is a huge expanse of open heathland and oak woodland. There is a pay car park by the RSPB information centre and from there it is about a 2km walk to Shipstal Beach. There are numerous walks around the heathland and viewpoints and hides are located at various points. The RSPB website claims that, in summer, Dartford warblers nest in the heather and nightjars fly at dusk. The beach at Shipstal Point is a good spot to watch watch thousands of wading birds, ducks and geese. Ospreys can be seen on migration in late summer and in autumn.

(Hot drinks machine at information centre.)

Poole Shore Road Beach SZ051885, BH13 7PR

Shore Road is continuous with Sandbanks beach and very similar to it. Again, it is family friendly with very good facilities and a long stretch of sand – though there are a few pebbles – and access from the car park is easy.

Canford Cliffs Chine SZ061894, BH13 7BN (or use Shore Road)

As it requires a little more effort to reach Canford Cliffs Chine than Shore Road and Branksome Chine beaches, it may be a quieter than its neighbours. Like them it is a sandy, family friendly beach with good facilities. It can be approached along the promenade that links all the Poole and Bournemouth beaches. Alternatively, use the Western Road car park on Canford Cliffs and follow the stepped path down.

Branksome Dene Chine SZ068900, BH13 6JT

Another fine, sandy beach, with good access and facilities, Branksome Dene Chine differs from neighbouring Branksome and Alum Chines in permitting dogs year round. However, it doesn't have lifeguard cover, so swimmers should use the beaches that do.

Branksome Chine SZ065897, BH13 6LP

The car park, toilets, shop and café are right by the beach at Branksome Chine. Again, it is a fine, sandy beach, with very good facilities and ideal for families.

Bournemouth - Alum and Durley Chine SZ074903, BH4 8AN (Alum) or SZ078905, BH4 8AA (Durley)

Very similar to Branksome Chine, Alum and Durley Chines are sandy, family beaches in the Bournemouth series with handy parking and facilities. Again, use the posted beach maps to verify the zones for swimming and other activities and to locate the dog exercise area. This is Middle Chine, between Alum and Durley Chines.

Bournemouth Central Beach SZ086908, BH2 5DL (closest one)

Bournemouth has long been a leading resort and Central Beach has the classic ingredients of the traditional British seaside. These include the pier with its theatre; amusement arcades and a wide range of seafront bars, cafes, restaurants and snack bars. There are also an aquarium; a fun fair; boat and open top bus trips; deck chairs and chalets. Not far away are Bournemouth's many shops; an art gallery and museum; plus the Pavilion and BIC theatres. With all these attractions and easy access from the car parks, Central tends to be the busiest beach in Bournemouth – and yet early or late in the day or out of season it has all the romance of remoter beaches.

P

Boscombe Beach SZ111912, BH5 1BL or SZ112913, BH5 1BG

Boscombe Beach is sandy and easily accessed from parking on Undercliff Drive and at Overstrand car park. The beach stretches east and west of Boscombe Pier with lifeguard stations on both sides. As elsewhere along Bournemouth's beaches, visitors should swim between the red and yellow flags in the lifeguarded areas and enjoy watersports in the designated zones. Boscombe is popular for both surfing and kayaking and there are places to buy and hire surfing equipment and gain instruction. There is also a man made surf reef east of the pier which acts like a ramp, pushing the waves upwards and giving experienced surfers a long ride. Like Central Pier, Boscombe Pier is part of Bournemouth's seaside heritage and has panels explaining its history. For the less energetic, sunbeds, windbreaks and parasols may be hired. Other nearby attractions include Boscombe Gardens, a mini golf course, a children's play area and a sports complex.

Bournemouth - Fisherman's Walk SZ130913, BH5 2GL (or as Boscombe)

Fisherman's Walk is east of and similar to Boscombe Beach, with plenty of golden sand. There is a lifeguarded area for swimming, plus a surfboard and watercraft zone. Fisherman's Walk can be accessed on foot from Boscombe Pier, but there is free parking on the Overcliff Drive above the beach itself, with access via the Fisherman's Cliff Lift or by ramped path. There are toilets and a café on the beach; with further toilets, café, pub, play park and crazy golf course on the Overcliff, which is also a local nature reserve. Although dogs are banned on the main part of the beach, they are permitted between Fisherman's Walk and neighbouring Southbourne.

 (free)     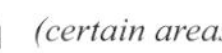 (certain areas) 

Southbourne Beach SZ146912, BH46 4BD

Southborne's sandy beach is an easterly continuation of Fisherman's Walk, though with rather more pebbles. Access is from a handy beach front car park or free roadside parking a little further away. There is a lifeguarded swimming zone and opportunities for surfing and watersports such as kayaking in the surfing/watercraft zone. Dogs are banned from the main part of Southbourne, but permitted in a zone between Southbourne and Fisherman's Walk and eastwards to Hengistbury Head.

Right: A surfer at Boscombe.

Hengistbury Head SZ163912, BH6 4EN

The eastern end of Poole Bay, Hengistbury Head has over 3km of sand and pebble beach and a network of paths inland. A place of great natural beauty it is best explored on foot, being also a Nature Reserve and an SSSI, with a wide range of plants and birds, notably skylarks. Occupied since the Old Stone Age, Hengistbury Head is an important archaeological site too with Iron Age defences (the Double Dykes) surviving from its period as a prehistoric port. Hengistbury Head may be easily accessed from the pay and display car parks at Solent Beach and at the road end towards the headland – where there is a café and toilets and near which there is also some free (limited time) on road parking. Alternatively, take the ferry from Mudeford Quay (page 45) to the far eastern end of Hengistbury Head. Dogs are allowed on the beach and on paths, but please keep them on leads and under strict control near nesting birds and other wildlife.

Mudeford Beach SZ183917, BH23 4AB

Mudeford Quay offers two beaches from one car park plus good facilities. North-eastwards is a small sand and pebble beach. Continuous with the larger Avon, Friars Cliff and Highcliffe beaches, it is good for exercising dogs, but not for swimming due to the tides and currents. By taking the Mudeford Ferry (07968 334441) from the southern end of the car park, where the pub, shop, café and toilets are located, you can enjoy Mudeford Sandbank beach, an unspoilt sandy beach designated for swimming and continuous with Hengistbury Head (page 44). Fishing trips and scenic boat trips are also offered from Mudeford Quay.

Avon Beach SZ188922, BH23 4AN

Avon is a sandy beach with some pebbles, popular with families and with easy access from the car park. It is suitable for swimming and watersports, but please keep to the designated zones – swimming at the Friars Cliff end of the beach, windsurfing and other watersports near the car park. Also, beware strong currents and the danger of being cut off by the tide.

Friars Cliff Beach SZ195928, BH23 4TA

An eastward continuation of Avon Beach, Friars Cliff is a beach of sand with some pebbles. It is quite easily accessed from car parks off South Cliffe Road and Seaway Avenue and zoned for bathing with lifeguards. Further east, Steamer Point is zoned for watersports, whilst the beach below Highcliffe Castle is designated for bathing.

Highcliffe Beach SZ216933, BH23 5DG or SZ203932, BH23 4LD (castle)

Dorset's easternmost beach, Highcliffe is a long stretch of sand and shingle, zoned for swimming and watersports with seasonal lifeguard cover. (Please heed warnings of rock falls and undercurrents). The cliff top car park off Wharncliffe Road affords moderately easy access and has toilets and a café. Dogs are only permitted on a limited zone of the beach. One mile to the west is Highcliffe Castle, a restored early 19th century mansion with visitor centre and toilets. Its car park (maximum stay four hours) gives another approach to the beach.

(in a specific zone)

The author's recommendations

Dorset's beaches and coves offer scope for a wide range of activities. Below are some personal favourites, but please don't take this as a definitive list! Also, please keep safety in mind; especially on beaches where there are rock falls, strong tides and currents or a steep shelf.

Fossils and Fossil Collecting: Lyme Regis and Museum; Charmouth and Heritage Coast Centre; Seatown; Portland Museum; Lulworth Cove and Museum; The Etches Collection, Kimmeridge; *Square and Compass* at Worth Matravers.

Coastal walks and Scenery: Charmouth to Seatown including Golden Cap; Portland Bill; Durdle Door to Lulworth Cove; Lulworth Cove to Fossil Forest and Worbarrow; Studland to Handfast Point and Old Harry Rocks; Worth Matravers to Winspit and St Adhelm's Head; Durlston Country Park, Swanage.

History: Lyme Regis; Portland Castle; Weymouth; Hengistbury Head.

Family Fun: Lyme Regis; West Bay; Abbotsbury Children's Farm; Weymouth; Bowleaze Cove; Swanage; Poole; Bournemouth.

Swimming: Lyme Regis; Weymouth; Studland; Poole; Bournemouth.

Beach Fishing: Chesil beaches.

Boat trips (including fishing): Lyme Regis; West Bay; Weymouth; Swanage; Poole; Bournemouth; Mudeford.

Far From the Madding Crowd: Eype; Cogden; East Fleet; Mupe Bay; Brownsea Island; Shipstal Point; Hengistbury Head.

Watersports: Diving at Chesil Cove; Church Ope Cove and Swanage; kayaking at Studland; windsurfing at Portland; snorkeling at Kimmeridge; surfing and kitesurfing at Bournemouth; sailing at Weymouth, Portland and Studland.

Wildlife and Birdwatching: Cogden; Abbotsbury Swannery; Chesil Bank Nature Reserve; Ferry Bridge; Wyke Regis; Portland Bill; Radipole Nature Reserve, Weymouth 01305 778313, www.rspb.org.uk; Kimmeridge; Durlston Country Park, Swanage; Studland Heath; Brownsea Island; RSPB reserve at Arne; Hengistbury Head Nature Reserve.

Good dog beaches: Many beaches allow dogs, and almost all do in winter. Great places to walk dogs include Durdle Door, Kimmeridge, Worbarrow and Hengistbury Head. For a family beach day including the dog try Bowleaze Cove or Lulworth.

Inspiring Places Publishing publishes illustrated guides on Dorset. All titles can be ordered online at:
www.inspiringplaces.co.uk
or can be purchased at many bookshops and tourist outlets throughout the county, including most Tourist Information Centres. A full list of titles is given below.

Ancient Dorset 40pp £3.99
Fossils and Rocks of the Jurassic Coast 40pp £3.99
All about - The Jurassic Coast 48pp £4.99
Tales of Historic Dorset 48pp £4.99
Dark Age Dorset 40pp £3.99
The Life and Works of Thomas Hardy 48pp £4.99
Tales of the Dorset Coast 48pp £4.99
A brief guide to Purbeck 40pp £3.99
A brief guide to Weymouth, Portland and Dorchester 40pp £3.99
A brief guide to Sherborne, Shaftesbury and Blandford 32pp £3.99
Day Tours in the East of Dorset 32pp £3.99
A Guide to the Beaches and Coves of Dorset 48pp £4.99
Jurassic Coast Fossils 40pp £3.99
Walking West Dorset 48pp £4.99
Purbeck Walks 40pp £3.99
Legends and Folklore of Dorset 40pp £3.99
Secret Dorset 44pp £3.99
The Railway Heritage of Dorset and Somerset 48pp £4.99
Great Houses and Gardens of Dorset 40pp £3.99

Front cover: Man O' War Bay near Lulworth.
Rear cover: East Beach, West Bay.